HOLY
WAYS
IN
HOLIDAYS

HOLY WAYS
IN
HOLIDAYS

REMEMBERING THE GUEST OF HONOR

JERRY CROSSLEY
AUTHOR OF *THE SEEN AND THE UNSEEN*

REDEMPTION❦PRESS

Published by Redemption Press, PO Box 427, Enumclaw, WA 98022

ISBN 13: 978-1-63232-036-0
Library of Congress Catalog Card Number: 2012914484

DEDICATION

More than just being my wife for half a century,
Julie Roberts Crossley
has been, first and foremost, a handmaid of the Lord,
exemplifying the radiant beauty of Christian
womanhood.

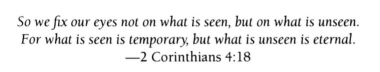

So we fix our eyes not on what is seen, but on what is unseen.
For what is seen is temporary, but what is unseen is eternal.
—2 Corinthians 4:18

CONTENTS

ACKNOWLEDGMENTS

I WANT TO express my gratitude to the following:

Heidi Ruiz, widow of Joe Space (see chapter 1), who loyally stood by her husband, sharing his suffering and his triumphant faith in Christ, and who graciously gave me permission to share his story with you.

David Lusch (see chapter 9), whose own simple act of kindness powerfully touched us all.

David Gabl (see chapter 10), my son-in-law, who eloquently offered a vivid illustration of Incarnation.

Stanley Dlugosz (see chapter 13), my life-long friend who taught me about forgiveness.

Janet Neill, my typist, without whom there would be no manuscript in the first place.

Our son, Paul Allen Crossley, for his technical support. Every time we sat at the computer and screamed in frustration, Paul magically appeared and rescued his aged parents.

The Editorial Staff who knew what I wanted to say and helped me say it better.

A whole host of people whose deep spirituality shaped and molded my own spirit. "Therefore, since we are surrounded by such a great cloud of witnesses, let us throw off everything that hinders and the sin that so easily entangles, and let us run with perseverance the race marked out for us. Let us fix our eyes on Jesus, the author and perfecter of our faith, who for the joy set before him endured the cross, scorning its shame, and sat down at the right hand of the throne of God" (Heb. 12:1-2).

For each of these great people of God, I give Him thanks.

Truly you are a God who hides himself,
O God and Savior of Israel.
—Isaiah 45:15

Now to the King eternal, immortal, invisible, the only God,
be honor and glory for ever and ever. Amen.
—1 Timothy 1:17

Immortal, invisible, God only wise,
In light inaccessible, hid from our eyes.
Most blessed, most glorious, the Ancient of Days,
Almighty, victorious—Thy great name we praise!
Great Father of glory, pure Father of light,
Thine angels adore Thee, all veiling their sight;
All praise we would render: O help us to see
'Tis only the splendor of light hideth thee!
—Walter Chalmers Smith,
"Immortal, Invisible"

By faith [Moses] left Egypt, not fearing the king's anger;
he persevered because he saw him who is invisible.
—Hebrews 11:27

By faith we understand that the universe was formed at
God's command, so that what is seen was not
made out of what was visible.
—Hebrews 11:3

I ask no dream, no prophet ecstasies,
No sudden rending of the veil of clay,
No angel visitant, no opening skies;
But take the dimness of my soul away.
—George Croly, "Spirit of God,
Descend Upon My Heart"

We live by faith, not by sight.
—2 Corinthians 5:7

*Now faith is being sure of what we hope for and
certain of what we do not see.*
—Hebrews 11:1

*And, Lord, haste the day when my faith shall be sight,
The clouds be rolled back as a scroll.*
—Horatio G. Spafford,
"It Is Well With My Soul"

*You will seek me and find me when you seek me with all
your heart. I will be found by you.*
—Jeremiah 29:13-14

*Now we see but a poor reflection as in a mirror;
then we shall see face to face.*
—1 Corinthians 13:12

*He is a God who works "behind the scenes";
He is also a God who, unseen, works behind the "seens."*
—Jerry Crossley

*Faith is believing what you do not see, and the reward of
faith is seeing what you believe.*
—Huston Smith, "Why Faith Matters Today"

*We believe in one God, the Father, the Almighty, maker of
heaven and earth, of all that is, seen and unseen.*
—The Nicene Creed

PREFACE

L IKE MOST PEOPLE, I love holidays. After all, holidays are occasions for partying! Yet I have noticed that when people celebrate the holidays, they often don't realize *what* they are celebrating. That is why the holidays so often degenerate into holidaze. Eventually, the celebrants are simply celebrating the act of celebrating! However, if you look deeply, you will find "the reason for the season."

The apostle Paul wrote, "So we fix our eyes not on what is seen, but on what is unseen. For what is seen is temporary, but what is unseen is eternal" (2 Cor. 4:18). Paul was saying, in effect, "When you look behind the 'seens,' you will see God." So, this season, let your soul stand on tiptoe so you can discover the holy ways in the holidays. When you do, each way will become a pathway to blessing.

CHAPTER 1

THANKFUL IN ALL CIRCUMSTANCES?

THANKSGIVING

We live by faith, not by sight.
—2 Corinthians 5:7

ALL OF US love Thanksgiving, with its cornucopia of food and drink, friends and family, feasting and football. Yet deep down we recognize Thanksgiving is more than a *holiday*; it's a *holy* day. It's a day on which we worship and celebrate by being thankful. We thank God for the possessions He has given us, the friendships He has provided, and all the other gifts He has bestowed on us.

It's easy to be thankful when we can look back and see all of the ways God has blessed us. What is more difficult is to be thankful when we go through those terrible times in our lives when nothing seems to turn out right. We know that Scripture plainly states, "Give thanks in all circumstances, for this is God's will for you in Christ Jesus" (1 Thess. 5:18), but we have a lot of trouble with that verse.

I have certainly found this to be true in my life. My daughter-in-law had a brother named Joe who was her soul mate. Joe was a young man who was gifted with a fervent faith in Christ and who possessed unbounded spiritual energy. He had a heart for the poor and disinherited and wanted to develop an inner-city mission. He saw the vision with such clarity that he sold his home and moved his family into a drug-infested section of the city so he could witness and reach out to the least, the last, and the lost.

Unfortunately, it was not to last. When Joe went to a doctor's one day, the physician discovered he was already in the last stages of Hodgkin's disease. Eventually, Joe struggled through a bone marrow transplant, a subsequent remission, and a recurrence of cancer before succumbing to the disease. This young man who had so much passion to serve his Lord was cut down in the prime of life. All those whispered prayers and intense worship services had come to no avail. How could it be possible to give thanks in these circumstances?

Another time, I was serving a church in Croydon, Pennsylvania, when a sister church about seven miles away contacted me and requested my pastoral services. Their pastor had suffered a debilitating stroke, and they wanted me to cover for him. In their congregation was a twelve-year-old girl who had been battling cancer. She was presently hospitalized in Philadelphia, so I visited her several times, and we formed a strong bond of friendship. Even when I wasn't with her, I found myself thinking about and praying for her.

I don't have much medical knowledge. But as I visited her, it seemed that her morale was high and her condition was improving. On one Saturday morning, I sat beside her on her bed, mindlessly watching cartoons on television. Their crazy antics made us laugh over and over again. I had a heartfelt prayer with her and then returned home.

Later that afternoon, I received a shocking phone call. My little friend had died. Days later, I received a special note from her in which she thanked me for my visits and friendship. She had written it the previous week. I felt empty inside, like there was a big gaping hole in my heart. Give thanks in *all* circumstances? How?

We are not the first people to wrestle with the problem of suffering. More than 2,500 years ago, a psalmist named Asaph struggled with it as well. In one psalm he wrote, "Surely God is good to Israel, to those who are pure in heart. But as for me, my feet had almost slipped; I had nearly lost my foothold … when I saw the prosperity of the wicked. They have no struggles; their bodies are healthy and strong…. They are not plagued by human ills" (Ps. 73:1-5).

Asaph goes on to compare his situation to that of the wicked. He concludes that being faithful and good has been a huge waste of time, since he is still suffering and struggling. After all, why go on being faithful to a God who does not go on being faithful to you? Asaph complains, "Surely in vain have I kept my heart pure; in vain have I washed my hands in innocence. All day long I have been plagued; I have been punished every morning" (Ps. 73:13-14).

But Asaph doesn't allow himself to stop there and wallow in the depths of his misery. Although he is angry, he decides to go to God to gain a better understanding of why the wicked seem to prosper while the righteous suffer. He writes, "It was oppressive to me till I entered the sanctuary of God; then I understood their final destiny. Surely you place them on slippery ground" (Ps. 73:16-18). In other words, Asaph realizes the Lord gives the wicked enough rope for them to hang themselves.

God never answers the psalmist's complaints, but He does enlarge his understanding. Asaph sees beyond what is ordinarily seen and gets a glimpse into the unseen. He concludes the experience with this faith-building affirmation: "Yet I am always with you; you hold me by my right hand. You guide me with your counsel, and afterward you will take me into glory. Whom have I in heaven but you? And earth has nothing I desire besides you. My flesh and my heart may fail, but God is the strength of my heart and my portion forever" (Ps. 73:23-26).

Asaph's encounter with the Lord provides the key to being thankful in all circumstances. Although we will go through difficult and unfair situations at times, we must remember we cannot see how the Lord is using those circumstances in our lives. There is always more than meets the eye. So, in faith, we "fix our eyes not on what is seen, but on what is unseen. For what is seen is temporary, but what is unseen is eternal" (2 Cor. 4:18). We thank God for the work He is continually doing, even if we cannot see how it could possibly benefit us.

A woman named Hannah Whitall Smith shared her testimony of how she came to understand this principle and realize God is all-sufficient. Once, she was going through a strenuous time of doubting. She lived near a woman who was known to possess a profound spirituality, so Hannah went to her and asked a barrage of questions. The mature woman listened to Hannah intently, without interruption, and then declared, "But there is still *God*."

Hannah waited for a follow-up of some sort, but the woman said nothing more. It seemed she believed her simple statement was enough. Eventually, Hannah said, "You must have misunderstood me. I have all these complications in my life."

"I understood you completely," the woman said. "But I want to remind you that there is still *God*." That was her final answer.

Hannah left her house feeling shortchanged. There had to be more to it. At last she decided this woman, despite her renowned reputation for devotion and erudition, was simply incapable of handling such a complex case as hers.

Nevertheless, Hannah's personal problems were daunting enough that she decided to find a "legitimate" answer from the woman. So, she visited and revisited her mentor. Each time, she received the same line: "There is still *God*." Finally, Hannah realized this answer was complete in itself—that God is all-sufficient and all that she needed.[1] As Asaph declared, "My flesh and my heart may fail, but God is the strength of my heart and my portion forever" (Ps. 73:26).

When we struggle through times of trial, we need to hold on to the truth that God is all we need and He is always with us. A poignant tale told by S. D. Gordon of a faithful old woman whose memory had begun to fail illustrates this idea. There had been a time when this woman had the whole Bible committed to memory, but toward the end of her life she found all that slipping away. The woman's favorite verse was 2 Timothy 1:12, "For I know whom I have believed, and am persuaded that he is able to keep that which I have committed unto him against that day" (KJV). As time passed, her memories eroded until only a piece of that verse remained: "That which I have committed unto him." Finally, as she approached death, she could remember only one single word of that verse: "Him." She kept repeating it: "Him … Him … Him." In that single word, she found the entire Bible.[2]

As I consider what I am personally thankful for this Thanksgiving, I realize I am most thankful for the Lord Himself. Everything else in my life can be taken away except for Him. Paul assures us, "What shall we then say to these things? If God be for us, who can be against us? … Who shall separate us from the love of Christ? shall tribulation, or distress, or persecution, or famine, or nakedness, or peril, or sword? … Nay, in all these things we are more than conquerors through him that loved us. For I am persuaded, that neither death, nor life, nor angels, nor principalities, nor powers, nor things present, nor things to come, nor height, nor depth, nor any other creature, shall be able to separate us from the love of God, which is in Christ Jesus our Lord" (Rom. 8:31, 35, 37-39, KJV).

CHAPTER 2

MORE THAN WE EXPECTED!

ADVENT

I have been crucified with Christ and I no longer live,
but Christ lives in me.
—Galatians 2:20

G ROWING UP, IT seemed nothing ever happened in my neighborhood of Philadelphia. But when I was thirteen, some real excitement took place. A family moved into a row home, and the breadwinner was a National League baseball player whom the St. Louis Cardinals had just traded to the Philadelphia Phillies. His name was Harry Walker, but he would affectionately become known as "Harry the Hat" because of the way he continually adjusted his cap between pitches when he was at the plate.

On this particular day, my buddies were standing at the edge of the local park, gazing in wonder as the family moved into the home. When they saw me saunter toward them, they immediately accosted me. "Hey! Yo!" they said. "That house across the street is Harry Walker's. Just take your baseball up to his front door, ring the bell, and he will autograph it. No kidding!"

This seemed a bit brash to me, but the peer pressure from my friends compelled me to do it. So I went up to the front door and rang the bell. Mr. Walker met me and cordially invited me into his home. He took the baseball out of my quivering hand and started to autograph it. Out of the corner of my eye, I noticed a couple of other men. One was stretched out on the sofa, and another rested on a lounge chair. They were privately enjoying this autograph session.

"Hey kid!" they said. "You want our autographs too?"

I didn't know how to respond. I assumed they were Harry Walker's family members, and I was reluctant to offer them my baseball. "No thanks," I said. "Just Mr. Walker's!"

"Come on, kid!" they replied. "Be a sport! Let *us* sign your baseball too."

I was more than a little intimidated by their persistence, so I finally offered them my baseball. They signed it: "Marty Marion" and "Stan Musial." I was amazed. These were two of professional baseball's immortals. I had come to the front door looking for a gift—an autograph from Harry Walker—but I had received something greater than I could have ever imagined.

Sometimes in life we get more than we expect. Like most other kids, I always anticipated the arrival of Christmas morning. My mother would wake up my sister and me and, still in our pajamas, we would tiptoe down the stairs in hushed silence, as if on the edge of a great mystery. The Christmas lights on the tree would be illuminated, providing a soft, ethereal, other-worldly atmosphere. Then our gaze would fix upon the beautifully wrapped gifts arranged around the base of the fir tree.

It was always a joyful surprise when I opened a box and inside was something better than I expected. I remember one Christmas—probably my tenth—I received a precious package that contained a ten-karat gold signet ring. When I rubbed it, the ring shone lustrously. This was a gift to complement any ensemble, and I concluded I had just experienced the best Christmas possible.

Yet even though I enjoyed all the gifts I received on Christmas, the true meaning behind the holiday was lost on me. As I reflect on the Christmas celebrations at my local church—with poetry recitations, Christmas Carols, sandals-and-bed-sheets tableaux, angels with silver-foil halos and paper wings, and the inert doll in the manger—there was a distinct disconnect. None of it seemed to have anything to do with my day-to-day life.

By the time I reached my twenties, I could not find meaning or purpose for *anything* in my life. Everything seemed irrelevant—including me. At this low point I met Jesus and asked Him to be my Lord and Savior. I realized what I had been missing all this time. I saw the unseen. The greatest gift was not found at the foot of a Christmas tree but at the foot of a cross. By God's grace, I received more than I expected.

Whenever we come to the Lord in complete self-surrender, He always offers us a lopsided gift exchange. It's kind of like an old Abbott and Costello comedy routine I once saw. The smarter of the duo was dividing up a large pile of money, and each time he would count out a bill, he would keep more for himself. "One dollar for you, and one for me" he would say, giving himself and his slow-thinking friend a one-dollar bill. "Two dollars for you; and one, two dollars for me," he would continue, offering his friend one dollar while helping himself to two. "Three dollars for you; and one, two, three dollars for me …"

But with God, we experience the exact opposite. We come to Him and give of ourselves, with all our dysfunctions, and in turn He offers us Himself. He says, "One for me … and everything else for you." As the apostle Paul put it, we are crucified with Christ and no longer live of ourselves, but Christ lives within us (see Galatians 2:20).

Whenever we engage in a Christmas gift exchange and carefully pick out a gift we hope the recipient will appreciate, there is a chance we will get something good or even better in return. However, there is also a chance we will present our expensive, carefully selected gift only to receive, in return, a plastic spoon. But when we give of ourselves to Christ, we always receive something greater back in return. What He offers is brighter and more lustrous than a ten-karat gold signet ring—His presence in our very hearts.

How's that for a providential exchange. It's more than we expected.

CHAPTER 3

HOW DOES THE SAVIOR COME?

ADVENT

*Now when Jesus was born in Bethlehem of Judea in the days
of Herod the king, behold, there came wise men from the
east to Jerusalem, saying, Where is he that is born
King of the Jews? for we have seen his star in the east,
and are come to worship him.*
—Matthew 2:1-2, KJV

THE MEN WHO said these strange words were from the eastern end of the Fertile Crescent, in what is today probably Iraq or Iran. They were astrologers who read the sky like a book and discovered the destinies of men and nations in the arrangement of constellations and configurations of stars. On this occasion, they had seen something that told them a person of cosmic importance had just come into the world.

So they followed one magical star until its radiant light hung suspended, like a chandelier, over the town of Bethlehem. They found the home of Mary and Joseph, entered in, and presented their gifts to the holy family (see Matthew 2:11). It has always amazed me that these magi, who were seasoned travelers, could gaze upon this young child and conclude that here was the promised Savior for whom they had been searching. They recognized the need for a Savior and were willing to follow the star for miles until they found Him. He came to them in the form of a child.

Sadly, there are plenty of people who never feel this need for a Savior. I think of the relatives on my mother's side who grew up without any spiritual guidance or religious instruction. My cousins were very blasé when it came to faith issues. They didn't find a Savior because they weren't looking for one, and they weren't looking for one because they didn't feel the need for one. As far as they were concerned, there was nothing from which they needed to be saved. In contrast, there are some who recognize just how great their need is of a Savior. Like the psalmist, they say, "Out of the depths have I cried unto thee, O LORD. Lord, hear my voice" (Ps. 130:1-2, KJV). They need a Savior to reach down and lift them up. And that's how He comes.

Many of the people whom Jesus encountered when He began His ministry called out to Him in the same way. One time, Jesus and His disciples walked along the road that led from Jericho to Jerusalem. Crowds had lined the road, hoping not only to catch a glimpse of this rabbi, but also to catch the words of His teaching. Typically, whenever a teacher walked with his students, he taught them as they went along. He wouldn't say, "Let's just walk in silence until we reach the next tree up there." The crowds knew this, and they wanted to overhear Jesus' words. But on this occasion they couldn't because of one loud-mouthed beggar on the side of the road who kept hollering, over and over, "Jesus, Son of David, have mercy on me!" (Mark 10:47).

This man, whose name was Bartimaeus, was perhaps the only one in the crowd who could not physically see Jesus. He was blind, and because he was blind, he was obliged to be a beggar. It was probably not his first choice of vocations. On this particular day he had not come in the hope of seeing Jesus, but in the hope Jesus would see *him*. This would be his last chance, for Jesus was on His way to Jerusalem to die. As the blind poet Fanny Crosby wrote, "Pass me not, O gentle Savior. Hear my humble cry; while on others Thou art calling, do not pass me by."[1]

Many in the crowd told Bartimaeus to be quiet, but Jesus stopped and asked for the man to be brought to Him. So they called to the blind man and said, "Cheer up! On your feet! He's calling you."

Bartimaeus threw his cloak aside, jumped to his feet and came to Jesus.

When he arrived, Jesus asked, "What do you want me to do for you?"

The blind man replied, "Rabbi, I want to see."

Jesus told him to go, for his faith had healed him. Immediately Bartimaeus received his sight and followed Jesus along the road (see Mark 10:49-52). How had the Savior come to him? As a passerby!

Many years later, a proud and self-willed Pharisee named Saul of Tarsus was making it his business to harangue and harass the first followers of Jesus. As he traveled to the city of Damascus to uproot the Christians there, he had a personal encounter with the Savior. Jesus, resurrected from the dead and ascended into heaven, came to Saul cataclysmically as the Lord. Saul later described the scene: "About noon ... as I was on the road, I saw a light from heaven, brighter than the sun, blazing around me and my companions. We all fell to the ground, and I heard a voice saying to me in Aramaic, 'Saul, Saul, why do you persecute me?' ... Then I asked, 'Who are you, Lord?'" (Acts 26:13-15).

It has been noted Saul inadvertently answered his own question when he called Jesus, "Lord." He hadn't met Jesus in a crèche, as did the shepherds (see Luke 2:16), but in the crash of a thunderous voice from heaven; not in the flesh as did His disciples, but in the flash of a blazing light. The Savior comes in different ways to different people, but He always comes in a way that grabs our attention.

When Jesus makes His presence known, each of us can affirm, in the depths of our soul, "For God, who commanded the light to shine out of darkness, hath shined in our hearts, to give the light of the knowledge of the glory of God in the face of Jesus Christ" (2 Cor. 4:6, KJV).

When I was a little boy, I dreaded going to bed. My bedroom was upstairs, isolating me from my parents who remained downstairs.

And I was convinced the oppressive darkness was filled with phantoms, ghosts, zombies, ghouls, and—worst of all—"the Bogey Man." I would stare into the blackness of my room and see all kinds of scary hulks and shapes, menacing and ready to pounce. I would beg my parents to leave the light on in the hallway. I feared the darkness that might envelop me.

"For God who commanded the light to shine out of darkness …" (2 Cor. 4:6 KJV). It's like the father who took his little son to a Christian bookstore to purchase a picture of Jesus. The proprietor assembled a whole countertop of paintings. The little boy rejected all of them. None of the pictures represented what he wanted. The store owner finally grew frustrated and said with annoyance, "Well, just what kind of Jesus do you want, anyway?"

Somewhere, the little boy had seen a silhouette of a luminescent Christ that glowed at night. So he replied emphatically, "I want a Jesus that shines in the dark!"[2] That is the way each of us truly wants the Savior to come to us. We want a Jesus who shines in the dark. And, by God's grace, that is just what we get.

CHAPTER 4
I BELIEVE[1]
CHRISTMAS

When the angels had left them and gone into heaven, the
shepherds said to one another, "Let's go to Bethlehem and
see this thing that has happened, which the Lord has told us
about." So they hurried off and found Mary and Joseph,
and the baby, who was lying in the manger.
—Luke 2:15-16

THE SHEPHERDS IN this story did not trudge up the hill to find just any newborn baby. The angel had promised them, "For unto you is born this day in the city of David a *Saviour*" (Luke 2:11, KJV, emphasis added), and that was who they sought. They made that pilgrimage to find a Savior, and they found him lying in the manger.

Back in Israel's history, more than 1,000 years earlier, the Lord God had decided to deliver an enslaved people from their captivity and reveal Himself through their ensuing history. He addressed His spokesman, Moses, and instructed him to have each man in the community take a lamb for his family. The animal had to be without defect, and the people were to slaughter it at twilight. God then commanded the Israelites to take some of the blood of the animal and put it on the sides and tops of the doorframes of their houses. "On that same night," God said, "I will pass through Egypt and strike down every firstborn … and I will bring judgment on all the gods of Egypt…. The blood will be a sign for you on the houses where you are; and when I see the blood, I will pass over you" (Exod. 12:12-13). This was the origin of Passover.

A millennium later, the Virgin Mary brought into the world a little baby who represented the sacrificial Lamb of God (see John 1:29). This was the Savior whom the angel had announced to the shepherds, telling them, "Fear not: for, behold, I bring you good tidings of great joy" (Luke 2:10, KJV). The shepherds heeded the angel's instructions and went up to Bethlehem, and there they saw God's promises fulfilled. Whereas most people might hear only an empty silence, the shepherds could hear a choir of angels. Whereas most might look at the manger and see nothing more than a little baby, the shepherds could see the Lamb of God who takes away the sins of the world. They saw what few others could see.

Theologian Helmut Thielicke once observed there are certain individuals who mistakenly believe that what is ultimately important about Jesus isn't His *identity* but His *teachings*. They see Jesus as just a great moral teacher who spoke in parables and gave religious instruction that is of timeless value. "It's like the Greek mathematician Pythagoras," they state. "We don't really have to know all about his life in order to appreciate his Pythagorean Theorem." But does this line of reasoning make sense? Is it possible to detach the *parables* of Jesus from the *person* of Jesus Himself? Is it possible to detach the story from the storyteller?

Consider, says Thielicke, the parable of the Prodigal Son, in which Jesus offers a reassuring story about a younger brother who went astray but finally came back home and received a grand welcome. If we consider Jesus just a great teacher, could we conclude this is the way God will welcome us if we return to Him? Could we conclude there is a God somewhere who is willing to give us a second chance? No, we would regard the story as a nice little tale, but just a story. We can take the parable seriously only if we take Jesus seriously.[2] We can never see who Christ Jesus really is until we commit ourselves to Him. The commitment comes first and then the understanding, which is the opposite of our normal way of thinking.

When my son was maybe eight years old, I tried teaching him how to swim. I wanted him to know how to swim well enough so that if he fell into deep water he could bail himself out. My son reached the point where he could navigate the width of the pool in shallow water, but when I gingerly suggested that he try swimming the width at the deep end, he balked. "It's just the same distance!" I begged.

"Not vertically!" he shot back. "It's over my head!" I didn't push the issue.

Some time later, we were invited to swim in a neighbor's in-ground pool. I casually said to my son, "Why don't you give it a try?" I was thinking he might attempt swimming the width at the deep end. Instead, my son—Paul Allen Crossley—dove off the diving board and swam the *length* of the pool. What a leap of faith! I was so proud of him. Like Simon Peter, he had launched out into the deep (see Luke 5:4).

Now that our son had experienced swimming in the deep end, he understood the water could hold him up. In the same way, when we take a leap of FAITH (Forsaking All, I Trust Him) and fully commit ourselves to the Lord, we come to understand His supportive, though invisible, presence. As Deuteronomy 33:27 states, "The eternal God is thy refuge, and underneath are the everlasting arms" (KJV). We experience His presence and feel His arms beneath us when we live by faith, not by sight (2 Cor. 5:7).

The birth of Jesus Christ is more than simply a story; it is *His* story. In the past, God had spoken to His people through the prophets, but now He would speak directly through His Son (see Hebrews 1:1-2). It is more than just news; it is *good news*—"tidings of great joy," as the angel told the shepherds (Luke 2:10, KJV). It is more than just a ray of light at the end of the tunnel; it is light and life itself, for in Christ "was life, and that life was the light of men" (John 1:4).

As I mentioned previously, when I was a teenager I dutifully attended a local Sunday School and church, but my heart really wasn't in it. At that stage of my life, I was largely committed to my own interests and my own creature comforts. Not only was I not a Christian, but I had no faith whatsoever.

I had a best friend named Jack. We had been in high school together, and he was frequently in my home. He was brilliant, witty, and funny, and we spent a lot of time laughing together. But one afternoon when he came to see me, he seemed deadly serious, morose, and depressed. He wasn't his typical self.

Jack was a self-proclaimed agnostic, and he asked me if I thought there really was a God.

"Get that out of your head!" I immediately responded. "There ain't no [expletive] God!" I wouldn't even consider the possibility there *could* be a God. He would be too much of a major inconvenience. "Get that out of your head!"

A few weeks later, Jack was dead, apparently from a self-inflicted gunshot wound to the head. He had honestly come to me seeking help, and I had stood beside him at the crossroads of his life with absolutely nothing to say. I found myself staring into the abyss and the chaos of my own soul. I was terrified that life had no meaning at all. My own worst impulses filled me with revulsion. I knew I needed to be saved.

This tragedy, more than anything else, propelled me to wonder if there really was a Savior. I became desperate to know the answer. Eventually, like the shepherds, my search led me to the Lamb of God, the Savior of the world. That crucial encounter led me into the ministry. I knew I would encounter other troubled souls at the crossroads of life, and this time I wanted to be prepared to share God's grace. And I have been sharing the good news—the gospel of Christ—ever since. I've shared it in the hope that someone walking in darkness might see a great light (see Isaiah 9:2).

CHAPTER 5

THOUGHTS OF CHRISTMAS

CHRISTMAS

*And my God will meet all your needs according to his
glorious riches in Christ Jesus.*
—Philippians 4:19

AS MY MOTHER grew old and increasingly enfeebled by age, she also grew more apprehensive about the loss of her physical faculties. In a heart-felt prayer, she expressed her hope that she would always be able to experience the beauty and the passion of Christmas. And so she wrote:

> I look at the sights of Christmas, the happy faces, and the preparations for the celebration of Your day, dear Jesus. The lights, man's artificial creations, and God's own lights delight me. And I think, *If I ever lose my vision, may I still see Your star shining brightly in my consciousness.*
>
> I listen to the music of Christmas, the carols heralding Your birth, the chiming bells, and the sweet voices of the choir singers. And I think, *If I ever lose the ability to hear, may the soft cry of a babe in faraway Bethlehem always be with me, echoing in my silent ears.*
>
> I see the people walking, walking everywhere, frantically fighting against time to make Your day beautiful for their loved ones. And I think, *O Jesus, should my limbs ever fail me, may I remember Your life on earth and walk in Your footsteps in my mind.*

19

The beautiful things of Christmas are a joy to hold and to feel and to touch. And I think, *Dear Lord, should I ever lose the use of my hands to find through my fingers the miracle of Your creation, reach down with Your hand and touch me, and I will know Your love. Amen.*

—Ruth Koshland Crossley

I have often reflected upon my mother's wise words. As the chaplain of a retirement community, I had vivid reminders of those physical afflictions that will probably confront most of us as we experience the gradual diminishing of our faculties.

The secular holiday of Christmas offers a cornucopia of sights, sounds, colors, tastes, and fragrances. We don't want to miss any of it. Yet the sacred holy day of Christmas offers something even more precious, something that might not be immediately perceived: the power, presence, and promises of the Christ whose birthday we celebrate. We would not want to come to this feast and then miss the Guest of Honor.

Our body might suffer infirmities, but the Bible says,

Therefore we do not lose heart. Though outwardly we are wasting away, yet inwardly we are being renewed day by day. For our light and momentary troubles are achieving for us an eternal glory that far outweighs them all. So we fix our eyes not on what is seen, but on what is unseen. For what is seen is temporary, but what is unseen is eternal.

—2 Corinthians 4:16-18

CHAPTER 6

A NEW BEGINNING

NEW YEAR'S DAY

He who was seated on the throne said,
"I am making everything new!"
—Revelation 21:5

PEOPLE TEND TO get excited by the advent of a new year. Each New Year's Eve, huge crowds ecstatically accumulate in the squares of large cities around the world, sharing their huge hopes and huge dreams for the upcoming year. Despite the "hugeness" of it all, it really serves no purpose if the *year* has a new beginning but *you* stay the same. It's just a new year with the same old you.

As a young man, when the new year rolled around I always tried to make changes in my life to improve certain attitudes or behaviors. The only problem was that I tried to do it by myself without God. I would review my past performances and analyze my mistakes, miscalculations, and misjudgments, and then I would sit down and assiduously write out all of my New Year's resolutions, promising to change and alter my course. The resulting list was always impressively long and comprehensive, with enough paper to envelop any crime scene. It strikes me now that I was dealing merely with the symptoms but not the disease itself: my incorrigible self-centeredness. It wasn't long before I broke most of my resolutions and, subsequently, lost my resolve.

The Creator who designed us has higher hopes for each of us. We cannot change ourselves, but we can invite *Him* to change us. We cannot give ourselves a new beginning, but He can. As the apostle Paul wrote, "If anyone is in Christ, he is a *new* creation; the old has gone, the *new* has come!" (2 Cor. 5:17, emphasis added).

As previously discussed, in the Gospel of Matthew we read that the three magi who came in search of the King of the Jews were "from the east" (Matt. 2:1). No one is sure if they were Jews or Gentiles, or if they were from Babylon or Persia, or if there were just three of them or a dozen. We do know they were astrologers who had come to Jerusalem because they had seen a "star in the east" (Matt. 2:2), and they were wise men because they sought Jesus.

After hearing the prophecy that the Messiah was to be born in Bethlehem, the magi departed for that town and rejoiced when they saw the star stop over the place where the Christ-child was. There they found the child Jesus with Mary, His mother, and fell down and worshipped Him. They presented Him with "gold, and frankincense, and myrrh," and then, "being warned of God in a dream that they should not return to Herod, they departed into their own country *another way*" (Matt. 2:11-12, KJV, emphasis added).

The magi had seen the Unseen, and their lives could never be the same. They had to have a new beginning. Dr. J.T. Seamands wrote, when we likewise come to Jesus and pay homage to Him, we will always depart *another* way, turning away from our self-absorption onto a new pathway of unselfish love. It is simply impossible to meet the Lord and remain unchanged, because God is the God of new beginnings![1]

In the book *Every Common Bush*, Edgar T. Chrisemer tells a story about two outlaw brothers who were sheep rustlers. The brothers were caught, and after being tried and found guilty, they were sentenced to be branded like sheep. Two letters—*S* and *T*, for "sheep thief"—were burned into their foreheads.

One brother, unable to face the censure and contempt of the local citizenry, tried to run away to another country. It didn't work. Even there, many inquisitive people hounded him and asked what the letters meant. The brother isolated himself, and after years of frustration, he died bitter and forgotten.

The other brother reacted differently to his sentencing. He genuinely repented of his former deeds and decided to remain in his community to try to regain his neighbors' trust. As the years went by, he gradually earned their respect. Many years later, as the brother was nearing the end of his life, a stranger came to town and saw the letters on his brow. When he asked a townsman what the letters meant, the man replied, "I can't remember anymore, but I think they must mean 'SAINT.'"[2]

Because this brother had chosen to face his faults instead of running from them and had truly repented of his sins, he went from sheep thief to saint. In the same way, when we involve God in the process instead of trying to change everything on our own, He will lead us to become all that He wants us to be. The Lord makes all things new, which includes *us* if we make the decision to commit our lives to Him.

CHAPTER 7

THE GIFT YOU REALLY SEEK

EPIPHANY

Do not be afraid. I bring you good news of great joy that will
be for all the people. Today in the town of David a Savior
has been born to you; he is Christ the Lord.
—Luke 2:10-11

WHEN I WAS three years old, my mother took me Christmas shopping in downtown Philadelphia. We walked through Fisher's Park to the Fern Rock Railroad Station and took the train into Center City. We visited Gimbels and Snellenbergs department stores, ate lunch in the Horn & Hardart Automat, and then walked to Wanamaker's Department Store. The colors, lights, sounds, and fragrances mesmerized me.

One memorable day, my mother took me to see Santa. It was December 1940, and all of Europe was at war (America would join the struggle by the following Christmas). Given the truculent geo-political atmosphere, all of the toys for little boys seemed to have an association with the military—toy rifles, pistols, helmets, tanks, soldiers, and cannons. I stood sheepishly while each boy asked Santa for toy guns and a long list of other military-related items. Their mothers were all smiles, so proud of their young men.

When I climbed onto Santa's lap, I asked for a baby carriage and a doll. My mother was mortified. What was wrong with her son?

However, when Christmas Day arrived, those were the gifts I received. I was overjoyed. To this day, I can remember sashaying around the neighborhood, proudly pushing my little doll in her baby carriage as I called out to my gun-toting buddies to come and join the parade. My parents, out of their love for me, had given me the gifts I truly wanted.

Years later, when I was all grown up and in the ministry, I purchased an electric mixer for my mother. I thought she would find it to be a useful kitchen appliance, but it wasn't the gift she was seeking. I could read the disappointment in her eyes when she opened the gift, so I quickly said, "Mom, on second thought I'd like to return this. I'm going to make an exchange." That same day, I returned with a stunningly beautiful 14-karat gold bracelet. This time her eyes lit up with joy. She had finally received the gift she wanted.

At the time Jesus was born, the people of Israel were also eagerly seeking a gift. They were living under the oppressive rule of the Romans, and they were longing for the day when they would be free and Israel would again be one nation under God. Centuries before, God had promised He would send them a deliverer. Isaiah had written, "Behold, the Lord GOD will come with strong hand, and his arm shall rule for him: behold, his reward is with him, and his work before him. He shall feed his flock like a shepherd: he shall gather the lambs with his arm, and carry them in his bosom, and shall gently lead those that are with young" (Isa. 40:10-11, KJV).

The people were seeking this king who would be their shepherd, and God provided this gift by sending His own Son, Jesus, the "great Shepherd of the sheep" (Heb. 13:20). Jesus would later tell His disciples, "I am the good shepherd; I know my sheep and my sheep know me ... and I lay down my life for the sheep.... My sheep listen to my voice; I know them, and they follow me. I give them eternal life, and they shall never perish; no one can snatch them out of my hand" (John 10:14-15, 27-28). Later, over His cross a placard announced in Greek, Latin, and Hebrew, "THIS IS THE KING OF THE JEWS" (Luke 23:38).

Unfortunately, many of the people couldn't recognize Jesus in this way. Unlike the shepherds, they couldn't see this little baby lying in the manger would one day grow to be *their* shepherd. Unlike the magi who traveled from the East, they couldn't understand that the child in their midst was the great cosmic King who would one day command the loyalty and allegiance of their hearts and souls. He was right there before them, but because He didn't come in the way they expected, they couldn't see into the unseen and comprehend that He was the fulfillment of God's promise.

One person who was especially anticipating the fulfillment of God's promise was an old man named Simeon. He was a devout servant of God, and the Holy Spirit had revealed to him that he would not die until he had seen the Messiah (see Luke 2:26). Simeon knew prophecies such as Malachi 3:1, which states, "The LORD, whom ye seek, shall suddenly come to his temple" (KJV). So Simeon spent his days hanging out in the Temple precincts. Month after month and year after year, he waited in the Temple for the promised Savior to make His grand entrance.

I suppose Simeon expected to see a full-grown Christ enter the Temple. I picture him standing there expectantly, his eyes darting back and forth over the crowd, straining to catch the first glimpse of God's "anointed one." Then, one day, he happens to see a poor couple creeping through the arcade, cradling their infant son in their arms. Ordinarily, Simeon would have paid no attention, but when his gaze fixes on the baby, the Holy Spirit whispers, "This is the One! This is the One! Simeon, this is the gift you really seek."

Simeon immediately scooped the infant up, right out of the arms of the startled mother, as he proclaimed, "Lord, now lettest thou thy servant depart in peace, according to thy word: For mine eyes have seen thy salvation, which thou hast prepared before the face of all people; A light to lighten the Gentiles, and the glory of thy people Israel" (Luke 2:29-32, KJV).

Simeon did not allow his preconceived ideas to prevent him from hearing the voice of the Holy Spirit. He knew what he truly sought, and because he was willing to cling to the promises of God, he was able to look past appearances and see the true Messiah. In the same way, I pray that by God's grace you will be able to see into the unseen this Christmas and find the Gift you truly seek.

CHAPTER 8

A CONSECRATED LIFE

ASH WEDNESDAY

Like clay in the hand of the potter, so are you in my hand.
—Jeremiah 18:6

THE LORD WANTS each of us to live a "consecrated" life—a life that is set apart for His service. In worship liturgy, a consecrated cup, chalice or paten is not necessarily made of gold, silver, or any precious metal. In fact, on the surface it may seem ordinary, but it nonetheless has value because of the way in which it is used. It has been set apart for the Lord, which makes it valuable. The same is true in our lives. The apostle Paul wrote, we "have this treasure in jars of clay to show that this all-surpassing power is from God and not from us" (2 Cor. 4:7). As Christians, our value is not in what is seen on the outside, but in what is unseen inside our hearts.

We go about consecrating ourselves to God by putting our lives under new management—His! When we do, He becomes not only our Savior but also our Lord. But what does it mean to make Jesus the "Lord" of our lives? I remember struggling to explain this one time to a group of high school students at a Presbyterian winter retreat on the Delaware River. I was giving an address and urging them to invite Jesus to be "Lord" of their lives, but in response I was receiving just blank stares. It soon dawned on me that for many of them, the term "Lord" did not compute.

As I attempted to explain, I asked, "How many of you are members of a team?" Most of them, both males and females, raised their hands. "And whose orders do you follow?" I asked.

"The coach's!" they chorused.

"Suppose you disagree with the coach's instruction," I continued. "Who do you follow?"

"The coach!" they chanted.

"That's what it means to call Jesus 'Lord,'" I responded. "He's your coach. You refer every personal decision to Him." When we lead consecrated lives, we move Christ from the periphery of our existence to its vital center.

Unfortunately, many people are unwilling to relinquish this type of control to God—even among Christians. There are some who cannot envision how much God loves them, and thus they do not cherish His plans for their lives. They worry God waits for an opportunity to mess up their situations and rob them of their happiness, so they steadfastly cling to their own personal agendas.

In her devotional classic *The Christian's Secret of a Happy Life*, Hannah Whitall Smith relates a story about a friend named Sue who had these very fears about leading a life consecrated to God. Sue was afraid to seek God's will because she worried about what might go wrong if she released her own control. Hannah wanted to demonstrate how much God loved her, so she sought for a way to make her understand. She knew Sue was the mother of an only child, and she deeply loved her son, so Hannah decided to use the boy as a close-at-hand illustration.

Hannah asked Sue to imagine that her son said he would obey from now on and always trust her judgment. She asked how Sue would react. Would she seize upon this moment and use it to ruin her son's life and bring as much misery on him as possible? Of course, Sue emphatically denied she would do any such thing. Instead, she asserted she would be even more eager to bless his life in every way.

This response gave Hannah the opening she was seeking. Hannah asked her friend to stop and ask herself if she were more loving than God. When Sue replied no, she at last began to understand that in the same way her own son could trust her, she could trust her Father in heaven and yield herself completely to His will.[1] She began to see that God's plans were for her good and that she needed to give up the control to Him so He could begin to shape her for His purposes.

In Jeremiah 18, the Lord told the prophet to go down to the potter's house, where He would give him a message. Note that God didn't reveal His whole plan—just the next step. Jeremiah obeyed, and there he saw the potter working at the wheel. As the prophet watched, he saw the pot the man was making was misshapen; so the potter started over and began to form it into another pot. Just then, the word of the Lord came to Jeremiah: "O house of Israel, can I not do with you as this potter does? ... Like clay in the hand of the potter, so are you in my hand" (Jer. 18:6).

God knows how He wants to form us, but if we don't yield to His plans, we won't come out right. Often when we offer resistance, He will allow us to continue along our own course for a while, and then He will reform us into something else. This is why it is always best to yield control to God in the first place and allow Him to shape us according to His desires, not our own. The poet Adelaide Pollard wrote, "Have Thine own way, Lord! Have Thine own way! Thou art the Potter: I am the clay. Mold me and make me after Thy will, while I am waiting, yielded and still."[2]

In another story from *The Christian's Secret of a Happy Life*, Smith relates how she was once sharing her faith with a doctor who did not comprehend the importance of living a consecrated life. To help him understand, she asked how the doctor would feel about having a patient who brazenly said he had no intention of sharing his symptoms or taking the prescribed medicine. Furthermore, this patient would listen to this doctor's advice only if it made sense. Otherwise, he would go away. How would the doctor respond to this challenge to his integrity?

The doctor immediately said he would dump him as a patient. The only way he would treat the man is if he placed himself completely in his hands. Hannah told the doctor that he had just summarized the significance of consecration. Only in this act of self-surrender to God can we as humans find our joy and peace.[3] The clay can never be molded into something beautiful without first yielding to the hands of the Potter.

One man who understood this well was Dwight L. Moody. At a young age, Moody, who had no academic credentials, felt God was calling him to be an evangelist. One morning, he listened as a friend told him that he believed humanity had yet to witness what the Lord could do with a person who was totally committed to Him. Profoundly moved, Moody thought, I'll be that person. I'll be the one who completely surrenders his life. And he was. Moody became one of the most effective evangelists who ever lived. In the same way, God can do something special in *our* lives. We don't have to be Moody; we just have to be fully committed to Him.[4]

One day, I was conducting a worship service for the residents of The Shores at Wesley Manor, a United Methodist retirement community in Ocean City, New Jersey. As I spoke, I noticed all the residents were looking over my head at a crew of window washers. Later, as I looked at the excellent job these workers had done, I began to feel a little sad for them. I realized this crew's performance was measured on how well people *couldn't* see their work—how spotlessly clean the windows were and how easily people could see through them.

The same should be true with us. If we live a life totally consecrated to God, observers should not be able to see our work. Instead, they should be able to see right *through* us. We become transparent, and they are able to look right through us and see Jesus.

CHAPTER 9

SIMPLE ACTS OF KINDNESS

LENT

*I tell you the truth, whatever you did for one of the least of
these brothers of mine, you did for me.*
—Matthew 25:40

AN ELDERLY MAN rode a bus along a rural road in the Deep South. As he rode, he clutched a beautiful bouquet of flowers in his arms. Nearby sat a young woman who could not take her eyes off them. When the old man arrived at his destination, he got up and placed the flowers into her arms. "I saw you admiring these," he said, "and I just bet my wife would love for you to have them." The startled woman watched as the elderly man stepped off the bus and made his way to a cemetery, where he would tell his wife what he had done.[1] A simple act of kindness.

When Jesus was on earth, His entire ethic and way of life was focused on loving others and showing acts of kindness. At the final Passover Seder with His disciples, He said to them, "A new command I give you: Love one another. As I have loved you, so you must love one another. By this all men will know that you are my disciples" (John 13:34-35). Notice Jesus was not telling them to love others with *their* style of love, but with *His* style of love.

That's setting the bar pretty high. While our love often comes with strings attached, His love is unconditional and free.

Jesus explained this type of love in His parable of the Good Samaritan, which was prompted when an expert in the law asked Him what he needed to do to inherit eternal life. Jesus replied by asking the man what was in the law—what he knew God had commanded him to do. The man answered, "'Love the Lord your God with all your heart and with all your soul and with all your strength and with all your mind'; and 'Love your neighbor as yourself'" (Luke 10:27). Jesus told him that he had responded correctly, but the man wanted to justify himself, so he asked Jesus to define exactly who his "neighbor" was. Jesus answered by telling the parable:

> A man was going down from Jerusalem to Jericho, when he fell into the hands of robbers. They stripped him of his clothes, beat him and went away, leaving him half dead. A priest happened to be going down the same road, and when he saw the man, he passed by on the other side. So too, a Levite, when he came to the place and saw him, passed by on the other side. But a Samaritan, as he traveled, came where the man was; and when he saw him, he took pity on him. He went to him and bandaged his wounds, pouring on oil and wine. Then he put the man on his own donkey, took him to an inn and took care of him.
>
> —Luke 10:30-34

Jesus never answered his interrogator's original question. Instead, in good rabbinical fashion, Jesus answered the question with another question: "Which of these three do you think was a neighbor to the man who fell into the hands of robbers?" When the expert in the law replied it was the one who showed mercy, Jesus said to him, "Go and do likewise" (Luke 10:36-37). In asking the question, the man had hoped Jesus would *constrict* the boundaries and define those for whom he was responsible, but instead Jesus *expanded* them and eliminated the possibility of placing limitations on serving others.

We are to love *all* people and practice simple acts of kindness to *everyone* at *all times.* We can't permit our acts to be random or hit-or-miss. We must actively demonstrate Jesus' quality of love, not sporadically, but consistently and unconditionally, because in doing so we demonstrate our love to Him. Another parable that Jesus told emphasizes this point:

> When the Son of Man comes in his glory ... he will put the sheep on his right and the goats on his left. Then the King will say to those on his right, "Come, you who are blessed by my Father; take your inheritance, the kingdom prepared for you since the creation of the world. For I was hungry and you gave me something to eat, I was thirsty and you gave me something to drink, I was a stranger and you invited me in, I needed clothes and you clothed me, I was sick and you looked after me, I was in prison and you came to visit me."
>
> Then the righteous will answer him, "Lord, when did we see you hungry and feed you, or thirsty and give you something to drink? When did we see you a stranger and invite you in, or needing clothes and clothe you? When did we see you sick or in prison and go to visit you?"
>
> The King will reply, "I tell you the truth, whatever you did for one of the least of these brothers of mine, you did for me."
> —Matthew 25:31, 33-40

This parable reminds me of a story I heard about a young man living in the slums. He was trying to live out his faith and put his beliefs into action, but the more he tried, the more others made fun of him. One person contemptuously remarked, "Listen, if God really cared about you, don't you think He'd send someone into your life to help you?" The young man answered, "I think He does, but *someone* never remembers."[2] God gives us opportunities to show His love every day, but often we forget that when we serve the least of these, we are serving Him.

One time, I was leading a Bible study at a camp designed especially for grandparents and their grandchildren, and I wanted to share the parable of the Good Samaritan to show how we need to practice acts of kindness.[3] My wife and I were serving as program directors at this camp, and this particular summer my sister's friend Cheryl was attending and bringing her four-year-old grandson, David. The kids at our camp were from ages four through twelve, so David was one of the youngest. He was a bit intimidated, and he clung to his grandmother during our time together.

To make the parable more vivid, intense, and memorable, I decided to dramatize it and have the children play the different parts. I chose a twelve-year-old to play the role of the traveler journeying from Jerusalem to Jericho and three boys to play the "muggers" who would assault the unwary pedestrian. My twin grandsons, Eddie and Jimmy Gabl, were two of three bandits. They warmed to their part, and I had to caution them not to overact.

At the appropriate point in the skit, the hapless traveler crumpled to the floor and lay there whimpering while the other boys and girls, playing the parts of the assorted priests and Levites, walked apathetically past him. Little David, ensconced on the lap of his grandmother, intently watched. He slipped off her lap, and as the rest of us waited for the officially designated "Good Samaritan" to appear, he rushed to the side of the wounded victim. David began to stroke him and pat him—all he knew to do—in an effort to comfort him. He looked up at the people sitting around the circle and pleaded, "Help him! Help him! He's hurt!"

We sat, riveted to our chairs, conscience-stricken. This little boy, whom we had completely discounted as a contributing member of our community, had instinctively reached out to help with a simple act of kindness. We fought back our tears. It was a breakthrough event—an instant when eternity broke into human time. We would never forget this holy moment when time stood still and God's grace took center stage.

During this time of Lent, we need to focus on what we *don't* see (see 2 Corinthians 4:18). What we *do* see is the face of someone in need, but what we do not see is the face of Jesus. Each and every day of Lent truly becomes a holy day when we recall His promise: "Whatever you did for one of the least of these … you did for me" (Matt. 25:40).

CHAPTER 10

THE GIFT OF ATONEMENT

PASSION SUNDAY

While we were still sinners, Christ died for us.
—Romans 5:8

ONE WINTER WEEKEND, my family from Philadelphia was visiting us in Cape May Court House, NJ. We planned on watching a DVD of the Academy Award-winning film *Amadeus*, which had been voted Best Picture of 1984. We believed this film, with its intriguing story line and rich, classical music, would stimulate the imagination of our twin grandsons, Jimmy and Eddie. At age ten, they were especially attuned to music.

Unfortunately, that particular night Jimmy was out of sync with the rest of the family. He acted belligerent, selfish, and arrogant. His brother had waited on him and given him a slice of pizza, but Jimmy refused to thank him. When his parents gently urged him to do so, he pugnaciously challenged them. Defiant to the end, he was banished to his bedroom—no pizza, no soda, no movie, no camaraderie, no anything!

The rest of the family tried hard to watch the motion picture while Jimmy, the outcast, whimpered in his bed. Privately, I wondered how his daddy, my son-in-law David, would respond. As far as I could see, David had only two options: he could keep his son isolated from the family, or he could bring him back into our fellowship. The first choice seemed to represent judgment without love, while the second seemed to represent love without judgment (permissiveness). David found a third way. He went into Jimmy's room and lay down beside him in his bed. Instead of enforcing or annulling his son's punishment, he chose to *share it* with him.

I have heard it said that judgment and love belong together, and as I reflect on David's actions, I realize this is exactly what happened when God the Father sent Jesus into the world. Through the act of the incarnation, Jesus "became flesh and made his dwelling among us" (John 1:14), and then, "while we were yet sinners, Christ died for us" (Rom. 5:8, KJV). In our mind's eye and our heart's contemplation, we must permit ourselves to descend into the depths of Jesus' suffering so we can ascend to the heights of His love.

Just before Jesus' execution, He met with His disciples in an upper room. After taking the bread, giving thanks for it, and breaking it, He gave it to them and said, "This is my body given for you; do this in remembrance of me." In the same way, after supper He took the cup and said, "This cup is the new covenant in my blood, which is poured out for you" (Luke 22:19-20). The shadow of the cross was looming over Him, and He was about to be nailed to it. Through this final act of self-sacrifice, He made us at one with God. We call this act *atonement,* or, perhaps more correctly, "at-one-ment." Jesus paid the price for our sins so that we who were estranged would no longer be separated from our Father in heaven.

In his book *This Is Christianity*, Maxie Dunnam relates an incident that occurred during the course of his ministry. He had accompanied a young defendant to a court hearing. Instead of facing a jury trial, this young man stood before a judge, and Maxie stood with him. Maxie watched as the prosecution and the defense gave their arguments, and then the judge summoned the defendant to stand before her.

At that point, the judge launched into something of a lecture, and as she gathered steam, Maxie realized she was about to convict the defendant and sentence him to prison. So, he was surprised and taken off guard when the judge pronounced him not guilty. Maxie heaved a sigh of relief, but the judge was not finished. She reminded the accused that even though she had found him not guilty, he was not "innocent"—there was just insufficient evidence to convict him. She added that she personally did not believe he was innocent.[1]

In another courtroom scene described in the book of Romans, the apostle Paul writes, "What, then, shall we say in response to this? If God is for us, who can be against us? ... Who will bring any charge against those whom God has chosen? It is God who justifies" (Rom. 8:31, 33). In other words, God is the only one who can convict us or pardon us. Only He can finally declare us guilty or not guilty.

Furthermore, Paul adds, "Who is he that condemns? Christ Jesus, who died—more than that, who was raised to life—is at the right hand of God and is also interceding for us" (Rom. 8:34). As it turns out, the only one qualified to act as our prosecutor is our defense attorney. Through God's grace, He declares us not guilty—not because we're genuinely innocent, but because there is no evidence to convict us.

Why is there no evidence? Because He nailed it all to the cross. "He forgave us all our sins ... he took it away, nailing it to the cross" (Col. 2:13-14). On our own, there would have been no way for us to atone for our sins, but because Christ Himself "bore our sins in his body on the tree" (1 Peter 2:24), we are both "not guilty" and "not innocent" at the same time. Horatio Spafford wrote, "My sin—O, the bliss of this glorious thought! My sin, not in part, but the whole, is nailed to the cross, and I bear it no more. Praise the Lord, praise the Lord, O my soul."[2]

When we look at images of the dead Jesus hanging lifeless on the cross, He seems completely powerless. But again, we have to remember the distinction between the seen and the unseen. There is more than meets the eye. Seen through eyes of faith, Jesus represents the most dynamic power in the world—the power over death itself (see 1 Corinthians 15:54-57). All we have to do is confess our sin and trust in His forgiving love. John wrote, "If we confess our sins, he is faithful and just to forgive us our sins, and to cleanse us from all unrighteousness" (1 John 1:9, KJV).

There is a beautiful hymn called "Just as I Am" that is traditionally sung at Billy Graham Crusades when the speakers extend the altar call to their listeners. Over the years it has touched the hearts of thousands of people, not simply because the massed choir sings it so celestially, but because its sentiment echoes and reverberates in people's hearts and souls with resonating power:

> Just as I am, without one plea,
> But that thy blood was shed for me,
> And that thou bidst me come to thee,
> O Lamb of God, I come, I come.
>
> Just as I am, thy love unknown
> Hath broken every barrier down;
> Now, to be thine, yea, thine alone,
> O Lamb of God, I come, I come.[3]

When we come to God just as we are and lay our sins at the foot of the cross, He is faithful to forgive us. He declares us "not guilty" and covers our sins through the blood of Christ. The writer of Hebrews states, "When this priest [Jesus] had offered for all time one sacrifice for sins, he sat down at the right hand of God. Since that time he waits for his enemies to be made his footstool, because by one sacrifice he has made perfect forever those who are being made holy" (Heb. 10:12-14).

When we come to the cross, we haven't reached a dead end. Instead, we have arrived at the threshold of a holy way that leads all the way Home.

CHAPTER 11
THE ANOINTED ONE
PALM SUNDAY

*It was intended that she should save this
perfume for the day of my burial.*
—John 12:7

O N THAT FIRST Palm Sunday when Jesus entered
Jerusalem, "The whole city was stirred and asked, 'Who
is this?'" (Matt. 21:10). I have a hunch that many people
today, even church attendees, ask that same question. People come
to church regularly and still miss seeing Him. They listen attentively
to Scripture and still miss hearing Him. Their hearts are not open
to receive what their eyes are so anxious to behold.

It is much like the story of a little boy who had heard all about
the circus. One day, he saw a poster advertising a circus that was
coming to town, and the colorful descriptions stimulated his
imagination. This was a dream come true for him, and it was all
he could think about. He saved his allowance so he could attend
this fabled circus. When the night before the big show arrived, he
was so excited that he had trouble sleeping.

The next morning, the boy went to see the circus performers
parading down Main Street. He was dazzled by it all and enthralled
by the exotic lions, tigers, bears, elephants, camels, and beautifully

groomed horses. He watched acrobats, clowns, jugglers, and a wonderful marching band perform for the crowd.

As the last member of the circus band marched by, the little boy ran up to him, gave him his money, and turned and went home. It wasn't until years later that he realized he had never actually seen the circus. He had confused the parade with the Big Top and had missed seeing what he had come to see.[1] In the same way, many people today witness the celebration and hullabaloo of Palm Sunday but never get to *see* beyond it and behold the true Savior.

Even at the time of Christ, there were many people who could not see that He was the promised Savior. However, there were some who were able to grasp it. Mary, a young maiden, was one of those individuals. Before our Lord's birth, an angel came to her and announced that she would become the mother of the Messiah. In the Old Testament, that term cryptically referred to the One who would be *anointed* for a special task—the One who would suffer a sacrificial death and make atonement for the sins of mankind. As the prophet Isaiah had written centuries before:

> Surely he hath borne our griefs, and carried our sorrows: yet we did esteem him stricken, smitten of God, and afflicted. But he was wounded for our transgressions, he was bruised for our iniquities: the chastisement of our peace was upon him; and with his stripes we are healed. All we like sheep have gone astray; we have turned every one to his own way; and the Lord hath laid on him the iniquity of us all.
>
> Isaiah 53:4-6, KJV

Some time later, when Joseph, the man to whom Mary was engaged to be married, discovered that she was pregnant, he decided to quietly scrap the relationship. But then an angel visited *him* and reassured him the child in Mary's womb was, indeed, the Christ (see Matthew 1:18-21). The angel told Joseph this Messiah, the Anointed One, would save His people from their sins. Like Mary, Joseph was able to see into the unseen and understand what was happening.

John the Baptizer, a fiery prophet who had meteorically appeared on the scene, could also see beyond the seen. When Jesus had grown to manhood, He trekked down to the banks of the Jordan River where crowds of people were flocking to John to be baptized. When the prophet observed Jesus approaching, he cried, "Behold the Lamb of God, which taketh away the sins of the world" (John 1:29, KJV). John could immediately discern in Jesus the Messiah of whom the Old Testament prophets had foretold.

Nearby in the town of Bethany lived three close friends of Jesus: Mary, Martha, and Lazarus. Six days before Passover, Jesus arrived in this little town and attended a dinner given in His honor (see John 12:1-2). Jesus knew His death was at hand, and He had returned to Bethany to be with His good friends. At the same time, He was aware His adversaries were moving in on Him and closing the trap. Bethany was a scant two miles from their power base in Jerusalem, and Jesus knew He was on a collision course with them.

During the dinner, Lazarus's sister, Mary, slipped into the room bearing a vial of expensive perfume. Suddenly, she dropped to her knees, anointed Jesus' feet and wiped them dry with her long-flowing hair, filling the whole house with fragrance (see John 12:3). This was completely unconventional for a hostess to do, but in this moment her compulsion of love was stronger than the constraints of convention.[2]

More than anyone else in the room, Mary saw who Jesus really was: the Messiah and Suffering Servant about whom Isaiah had prophesied. She saw through the physical form before her to the unseen God. Warren Wiersbe notes, Mary, without embarrassment, was offering her funeral bouquet before the actual funeral.[3]

Judas Iscariot, the disciple who would betray Jesus, immediately objected. "Why wasn't this perfume sold and the money given to the poor?" he said. "It was worth a year's wages" (John 12:4-5). Judas was unable to see the gift for what it truly was, and he denigrated and demeaned Mary for its extravagance.

Today, our response to Mary's gift ultimately depends on our response to Jesus Himself. If we, like Judas, are skeptical about Him, we're likely to be skeptical about this ostentatious gift of perfume. However, if we are enamored with Him, as Mary was, we're likely to consider the gift appropriate.

It's interesting to see how Jesus deftly deflected Judas' protest. "Leave her alone," He said. "It was intended that she should save this perfume for the day of my burial" (John 12:7). In this way, Jesus was anointed for His death.

As Passover approached, Jesus left Bethany and, along with His followers and a multitude of pilgrims, approached the Holy City. He instructed two disciples to go into the village and bring a colt to Him, which He, in fulfillment of prophecy, would ride into Jerusalem (see Zechariah 9:9). As He did, "A very large crowd spread their cloaks on the road, while others cut branches from the trees and spread them on the road. The crowds that went ahead of him and those that followed shouted, 'Hosanna to the Son of David!' 'Blessed is he who comes in the name of the Lord!' 'Hosanna in the highest!'" (Matt. 21:8-9).

These words of acclamation were barely disguised political war cries. "Hosanna!" meant "Save us now!" or "Liberate us!" Furthermore, waving palm branches was like waving a flag of revolt. The crowds were hoping zealously for a political/religious liberation from the Empire of Rome. They looked at Jesus and saw a potential conqueror. They saw a King riding on a white horse and missed the Suffering Servant riding on a donkey.

Amidst the fanfare, the people could not imagine Christ came to Jerusalem to *die*. They could not see beyond what they could observe with their physical senses. So it was when the people in Jerusalem heard the commotion and asked, "Who is this?" the crowds of incoming pilgrims could only answer, "This is Jesus, the prophet from Nazareth in Galilee" (Matt. 21:10-11). Like so many others, they looked at Him but missed seeing who He truly was.

In Psalm 24, David describes a festival that was celebrated in Israel before the Babylonian Exile. During this celebration, a throng of devout pilgrims carried the sacred Ark of the Covenant outside the city walls and then joyfully escorted it back to the Temple gates. The pilgrims halted their procession before these imposing gates and said, "Lift up your heads, O you gates; be lifted up, you ancient doors, that the King of glory may come in" (Ps. 24:7). They said, in effect, "Hey! We're escorting the Lord God—the One and Only—into this city and into this Temple. You'd better stretch as wide as you can to receive Him. Your gates are too narrow and your doors too small for a God this big!" In contrast, half a millennium later, the people of Jerusalem saw the Messiah entering the gates and shamelessly asked, "Who is this?"

The hymn writer Georg Weissel wrote:

> Lift up your heads, ye mighty gates;
> Behold, the King of glory waits;
> The King of kings is drawing near;
> The Savior of the world is here!
>
> Fling wide the portals of your heart;
> Make it a temple, set apart
> From earthly use for heaven's employ,
> Adorned with prayer and love and joy.
>
> Redeemer, come, with us abide;
> Our hearts to thee we open wide;
> Let us thy inner presence feel;
> Thy grace and love in us reveal.[4]

Today, the same Lord who was with the Israelites wants to enter the innermost sanctuary of our hearts and make it His dwelling place. The question is whether we recognize Him and "fling wide the portals of our heart." Will we open our hearts to receive what our eyes are so anxious to behold?

CHAPTER 12

WHY WEEP?

EASTER

"Woman," he said, "why are you crying?
Who is it you are looking for?"
—John 20:15

IT MUST HAVE been a dismal day. Beneath a darkening sky stood three crosses, and upon those crosses three men were stretched and publicly exposed in such a way as to invite savage mockery (see Luke 23:32-33). The victim on the center cross had a placard nailed above His head, bearing the words, "THIS IS THE KING OF THE JEWS" (Luke 23:38). The chief priests had tried to get Pilate, the Roman ruler of Judea, to write, "This man *claimed* to be king of the Jews," but Pilate had said, "What I have written, I have written" (John 19:21-22, emphasis added).

In a stroke of irony, Pilate had intended the placard to serve as a cruel joke on all the Jews he so despised. It also represented an effort on his part to demonstrate the fate that awaited any Jew who aspired or conspired to challenge the power of imperial Rome. "Look here!" Pilate was saying. "This is what will happen to you!"

One of the criminals crucified with Jesus joined in the crowd's ridicule. In his helpless rage, he hurled his own insults, saying, "Aren't you supposed to be the Messiah? The Liberator? The

Rescuer? Try rescuing yourself. And, while you're at it, rescue us!" (see Luke 23:39). But the other criminal recognized his own deep need for a Savior—not just in this world but in the world to come. As he looked at Jesus, he saw beyond what is transitory and into the eternal. He saw a King.

This man recognized the truth of the situation. "We are punished justly, for we are getting what our deeds deserve," he said. "But this man has done nothing wrong" (Luke 23:41). He had come to the King empty-handed, and he could not beg, borrow, barter, bargain, buy, or steal his way into the Kingdom. He literally did not have a prayer. So, he simply asked, "Jesus, remember me when you come into your kingdom."

Paul writes, "As the Scripture says, 'Anyone who trusts in him will never be put to shame.' For there is no difference between Jew and Gentile—the same Lord is Lord of all and richly blesses all who call on him, for, 'Everyone who calls on the name of the Lord will be saved'" (Rom. 10:11-13). The thief had nothing to offer but his faith—but it was enough. Jesus replied, "I tell you the truth, today you will be with me in paradise" (Luke 23:42-43).

I have often wondered how that dying man felt when he heard those words from Jesus. Perhaps the hymn "Rock of Ages" could well be his testimony:

> Rock of Ages, cleft for me,
> Let me hide myself in Thee;
> Let the water and the blood
> From Thy wounded side which flowed,
> Be of sin the double cure,
> Save from wrath and make me pure.
>
> Could my tears forever flow,
> Could my zeal no languor know,
> These for sin could not atone;
> Thou must save, and Thou alone.
> In my hand no price I bring;
> Simply to Thy cross I cling.

While I draw this fleeting breath,
When my eyes shall close in death,
When I rise to worlds unknown
And behold Thee on Thy throne,
Rock of Ages, cleft for me,
Let me hide myself in Thee.[1]

On the evening just prior to His crucifixion, Jesus had announced to His followers that He was "the way, the truth, and the life" (John 14:6). His disciples had heard what He said, and committed it to memory, but perhaps they did not believe Him. There was, however, one woman who believed in Him with all her heart. For her, Jesus was *her* way, *her* truth, and *her* life. He was her *whole* life. But now He was dead, and so was she. She was dead on the inside.

She stood outside His tomb, weeping, and as she wept she bent over to look into the grave. To her amazement, she saw two angels clothed in white, sitting where Jesus' body had been.

"Woman, why are you crying?" they asked.

"They have taken my Lord away," the woman replied, "and I don't know where they have put him" (John 20:13). In her mind, Jesus' enemies had dealt the final indignity—they had stolen His body. They would not even let Him rest in peace.

At this, the woman turned and saw a man standing there.

"Woman," he said, "why are you crying? Who is it you are looking for?"

Thinking him to be the gardener, she replied, "Sir, if you have carried him away, tell me where you have put him, and I will get him." Then the man said to her, "Mary" (John 20:14-16).

This man called her by her name. In joyful recognition that the one standing before her was Jesus, she cried out, "Master!" (John 20:16, KJV). How must she have felt? Perhaps the words of the ancient prophecy of Isaiah describe it best: "Arise, shine; for thy light is come, and the glory of the Lord is risen upon thee" (Isa. 60:1, KJV). Mary had come to the tomb empty inside, but there she had met Jesus, and with joy she could now proclaim, "I have seen the Lord!" (John 20:18).

In the end, each of us must come before the Lord with empty hands, for there is nothing we can offer Him but our very lives. Corrie ten Boom, author of *The Hiding Place,* tells the story of how her relationship with an eccentric aunt brought her to this realization. This particular aunt, whom Corrie called Tante Jans, was fascinated by the latest medical technologies and often consulted with her physician. One day, in the course of a routine examination, the doctor discovered she had diabetes. In that era, such a diagnosis was a death sentence. Eventually, the doctor concluded Tante Jans had less than a month to live.[2]

The family had an emergency meeting to decide how to break the news to her aunt so she would be prepared. After their discussion, Corrie's father decided the entire family should tell her together. As the members filed into the aunt's room, Tante Jans observed the expression on their faces and immediately guessed the purpose of their mission. They were coming to tell her that her life was over.

The family launched into their task, reminding her of all she had achieved, including her fundraising for charitable organizations. They wanted her to find consolation in these many accomplishments, and they tried to reassure her that she would not come to the Lord with empty hands. But Tante Jans dissolved in tears.

When at last she was able to reply, she told them that all these good deeds were like little baubles. Ultimately, each of us must come to the Lord with empty hands. None of us can bring anything to Him. But thank God we don't have to. He has done everything for us on the cross. And that, she told them, is all the assurance we need.[3]

CHAPTER 13

A MEAL BETWEEN FRIENDS

EASTERTIDE

He brought me to the banqueting house,
and his banner over me was love.
—Song of Solomon 2:4, KJV

WHEN I WAS a high-school teenager, I had a group of friends who clustered around me. Almost every day they would show up at my home, drape themselves over the furniture, and engage in small talk. Typically they would ask me, "What do you want to do tonight? Where should we go?" I enjoyed being the leader of this group. In spite of my diminutive stature, I never had to fear being bullied by anyone, because my entourage was with me wherever I went.

One day something happened to disrupt my privileged position in the pecking order. A young man named Stanley Dlugosz joined us. Stan was a star athlete at our neighborhood high school. In fact, he had been honored as the outstanding soccer player for the entire Philadelphia area—which included all of the public, private, parochial, and suburban schools. Stan was popular wherever he went. Now he was right here, with us.

The transfer of leadership was immediate. I felt abandoned. I pretended not to be personally offended—not to feel like a has-been—but I knew my position had been usurped. I soon began to search for ways to reclaim my lost prominence.

Someone once cleverly observed that whenever we want to lift ourselves above others, we will employ two tactics: stepping up and pushing down. Just like climbing a ladder, we will step up over our comrades with one foot while, at the same time, pushing them down with the other. I now engaged in that stratagem.

Stan announced that he had planned the perfect weekend for us. His brother Louie had access to a cabin in the woods, and Stan wanted to take us there. He said we could stay, buy food, and do whatever we wanted. We all contributed to a common fund and looked forward to enjoying the time away.

After the weekend was over, I suggested Stan had pocketed some of our funds. I implied (without knowing anything about the cost of food) that the items we purchased could not possibly have cost that much. I was deliberately deceitful. Even now, decades later, I am embarrassed by my behavior.

Stan was furious at the accusation and walked out. Truthfully, his only motive had been to provide a good time for the rest of us. Now our friendship was over, and deep inside I felt cheap and rotten. I stared into the abyss of my soul, but I was too ashamed to go back to him or my other friends and apologize. So I kept to myself.

Then, during Christmastime, Stan came to *me* and invited me to attend a New Year's Eve party at his home. "It won't be a party without you," he said. I felt chastened and exhilarated at the same time. Stan, the one who had been sinned against, had reached out to the one who sinned against him.

In the years to come, I frequently reflected on his actions. When I could not bring myself to come to him and ask for forgiveness, Stan had come to me. I had eaten of my friend's bread and lifted up my heel against him (see Psalm 41:9), and now he had magnanimously forgiven me. Our friendship had been restored.

In Jesus' day, hospitality was viewed as a sacred duty. Unlike in our society, where it is unusual for a family to sit down together at the same time for the same meal, in the culture of that time a meal created a sacred covenant between each participant—a life-long bond of friendship. Even today, when someone in the Middle East says, "There is bread and salt between us," that person means, "There is a sacred bond between us because we've shared this meal together." In a way, meals make deals.

In Jesus' time, when you ate a meal at a person's home, you demonstrated that you were allied with your host.[1] If anyone came by to threaten you in any way, you could be assured you were under the host's protection. The one who invited you and furnished you with dinner was duty-bound by the sacred laws of hospitality to defend you—even at the risk of his or her own life. It is for this reason that this mysterious line appears in Psalm 23: "Thou preparest a table before me in the presence of mine enemies" (verse 5, KJV). Even in the face of terrorists' threats, you were safe.[2]

Given this high regard for hospitality, you can see why in Jesus' day it was considered a shameful act of treachery to betray one's host. To share a meal with someone and subsequently betray that person was a terrible sin.[3] King David alluded to such a heinous act when he wrote, "Even my close friend, whom I trusted, he who shared my bread, has lifted up his heel against me" (Ps. 41:9).

This is what happened on the night of what came to be called the Last Supper. Jesus, after sharing a Passover meal with His disciples, walked with them to the Mount of Olives. When they reached the Garden of Gethsemane, He prophesied, "This very night you will all fall away on account of me, for it is written: 'I will strike the shepherd, and the sheep of the flock will be scattered'" (Matt. 26:31, quoting Zech. 13:7). That night Jesus was arrested, and all His "loyal" disciples—the ones who had shared their Lord's bread—"deserted him and fled" (Matt. 26:56).

We're right there with Jesus' followers, running out on Him. Jesus, the Host of the Lord's Supper, has spread a table before us and invited us to join Him. In so doing, He has offered to us the sacred bond of friendship and protection. As Solomon wrote, "He brought me to the banqueting house, and his banner over me was love" (Song 2:4, KJV). He wants us to enjoy a friendship with Him that will last forever.

However, like the disciples, after we profess our undying loyalty to Jesus, we take off (see Matthew 26:35). We break friendship with our Lord and go our own way. But Jesus doesn't leave us there. Instead, our Host comes to us and offers us a new meal so our relationship will be restored. This is exactly what He did for His disciples.

One morning after the crucifixion, Jesus stood on the shore of the Sea of Galilee in the pre-dawn darkness and watched His disciples fishing. At one point, He called out to them, "Friends, haven't you any fish?" (John 21:5). The disciples strained their eyes, but they couldn't make out the identity of the stranger standing on the beach. Finally, Jesus instructed them to throw the net on the right side of the boat, and when they did, the catch was so great they couldn't haul in the net.

The disciples quickly realized this stranger was the risen Lord. Jesus summoned them to come ashore, saying, "Come and have breakfast" (John 21:12). There before them was a fire of burning coals, and on the fire were some fish and bread. Jesus took the bread off the coals and *gave it to them*, and He did the same with the fish. In so doing, He wordlessly restored their friendship (see John 21:13).

When we look at this scene, we, like the disciples, have to strain our eyes to see what is really going on. We have to look past the temporary and fix our eyes on the eternal. This meal on the beach was more than just another breakfast—it symbolized the restoration of a friendship, a renewal of a relationship, and the enactment of an indissoluble sacred covenant.[4] Jesus, like my friend Stan, had chosen to reach out to the ones who had sinned against Him and restore the fellowship. He forgave them.

Today, Jesus is beckoning *you* to return to His presence. Again, He is inviting *you* to the Eucharist. Again, He is offering *you* a meal between friends. Will you accept His offer and join with Him around His table?

CHAPTER 14

THE FIRE THAT FELL

PENTECOST

Then the fire of the Lord fell and burned up the sacrifice.
—1 Kings 18:38

THE HEBREW PEOPLE were certainly grateful for the help the Lord God had given them. He had brought them out of their captivity in Egypt, led them through the wilderness, and ushered them into a good land—a land "flowing with milk and honey" (Exod. 3:8, KJV). Now, as they settled down to farm this land, they saw the native Canaanite population worshiping Baal, a fertility god, who, it was said, could make the rain fall and the crops grow.

Sure, God had said, "Thou shalt have no other gods before me" (Exod. 20:3, KJV) … but when in Canaan, do as the Canaanites, right? It certainly couldn't hurt. Of course they would continue to worship the Lord, but, on the side, they would also pray to Baal. That way, they would have all the bases covered. They could have it both ways!

Unfortunately for the Israelites, the prophet Elijah didn't see it that way. He spotted in this religious syncretism an abandonment of the Lord God, and their sinful acts filled him with righteous indignation. He determined he would show the people the one true

God—the same God who had said, "Do not worship any other god, for the LORD ... is a jealous God" (Exod. 34:14).

Elijah proposed that he and the priests of Baal each build an altar on Mount Carmel, lay a sacrifice upon it, and call upon their god. Whichever one answered by sending down fire to ignite the offering was the real god (see 1 Kings 18:23-24). The Hebrew people said, "What you say is good" (verse 24), and they all assembled to observe this little demonstration.

Elijah politely permitted the worshippers of Baal to go first. Their idol proved to be idle. Even though the priests implored his help, danced around, gyrated, and cut themselves with knives, nothing happened. Midday passed, and the priests continued their frantic pleading. "But there was no response, no one answered, no one paid attention" (1 Kings 18:29).

By the late afternoon, Elijah had seen enough. He stepped forward and prayed, and fire fell from heaven and consumed the sacrifice. Instantly, the Hebrew people recognized that Yahweh, the Lord their God, was both the Lord of history and God of nature. He was the one and only God (see 1 Kings 18:36-39). Charles Wesley later wrote, "O Thou that camest from above, The pure celestial fire to impart, Kindle a flame of sacred love on the mean altar of my heart. There let it for thy glory burn with inextinguishable blaze, and trembling to its source return, in humble prayer and fervent praise."[1] The fire that fell from heaven was a gift to the people to rekindle their hearts.

When Jesus came to earth, He also sought to rekindle the people's hearts. On the night of the Last Supper, He offered His disciples "a new commandment" (John 13:34, KJV). How exciting that must have been for them—they already had, at last count, more than 600 of them. Why would they need another? Yet here was Jesus, offering one more. But this commandment was different, because it summarized and fulfilled all the rest: "A new commandment I give you: Love one another. As I have loved you, so you must love one another. All men will know that you are my disciples if you love one another" (John 13:34-35).

Jesus had previously stated that all of the commandments hinged on just two: "Love the Lord your God with all your heart and with all your soul and with all your mind," and "love your neighbor as yourself" (Matt. 22:37, 39). Later, the apostle Paul caught Jesus' vision and stated to the Christians in Rome, "Let no debt remain outstanding, except the continuing debt to love one another, for he who loves his fellowman has fulfilled the law. The commandments, 'Do not commit adultery,' 'Do not murder,' 'Do not steal,' 'Do not covet,' and whatever other commandment there may be, are summed up in this one rule: 'Love your neighbor as yourself.' ... Therefore love is the fulfillment of the law" (Rom. 13:8-10). Likewise, to the Christians in Galatia he wrote, "The entire law is summed up in a single command: 'Love your neighbor as yourself'" (Gal. 5:14). The command was all-encompassing.

When the disciples shared the Last Supper with Jesus in the Upper Room, they must have wondered where they could get this kind of love. Where would it come from? As far as they could see, they could not generate it themselves. Like us, they were hard-pressed to love others with Jesus' kind of love. Like us, they quickly ran out of forgiveness, empathy, patience, and understanding. Like us, they ran out of juice. They could not see that this power of love would come as a *gift* from God. It would literally come out of the blue.

Later, when the twelve disciples and others of Jesus' followers were gathered together in a room in Jerusalem, that love fell upon them like fire from heaven:

> When the day of Pentecost came, they were all together in one place. Suddenly a sound like the blowing of a violent wind came from heaven and filled the whole house where they were sitting. They saw what seemed to be tongues of *fire*.... All of them were filled with the Holy Spirit and began to speak in other tongues as the Spirit enabled them.
> —Acts 2:1-4, emphasis added

Again, as in Elijah's day, the fire that fell from heaven came as a gift. Look and see through eyes of faith that the same God who had commanded them to love others was now supplying them with the love they needed to fulfill that command. He was enabling them, empowering them and equipping them with tools to perform the task He had assigned. As Paul would state, "God has poured out his love into our hearts by the Holy Spirit, whom he has given us" (Rom. 5:5).

As might be expected, when the people on the streets heard the noise and sound of celebration coming from inside the house, they wondered what was going on. The good news on the inside was about to spill over to the outside. At one point, Simon Peter stepped forward and addressed the crowd, assuring them, "The promise is for you and your children and for all who are far off—for all whom the Lord our God will call" (Acts 2:39). Peter was saying they too could experience Pentecost—just as we who are far off in time and space from that event can do as well. All we have to do is ask.

One time, I faced a difficult situation in a church I pastored. Typically, when I find myself in this position, I tend to rely on my "street smarts" and try to solve the problem on my own. However, in this case I discovered my own resources were woefully inadequate. Finally, I said to my wife, "There's nothing more I can do. If anything good is going to happen, the *Lord* is going to have to do it."

To this she responded, "He thought you'd never ask!"

In Luke 11:9-10, Jesus said, "Ask, and it shall be given you; seek, and ye shall find; knock, and it shall be opened unto you. For every one that asketh receiveth; and he that seeketh findeth; and to him that knocketh it shall be opened" (KJV). The problem is that so often we don't ask for God's help. It reminds me of a story I read about a young man who was attempting to move a heavy rock. He bit off more than he could chew, for that rock was just too big for him to tackle. He tried using all sorts of tools and techniques, but still it wouldn't budge.

Finally, the boy's father, who had been quietly observing his son's futile struggle, came over to him. "Son," he said, "are you having any trouble moving that rock?"

"Yes," the boy replied. "I've done everything I can think of."

"Are you sure you've done *everything*?" the father asked.

"Yes!" the son gasped in frustration.

"No, you haven't," the father replied. "You haven't asked *me*!"[2]

Ask—that's all we have to do. When we run out of our own resources, we can depend on God's. When we are unable to manufacture love for someone, we can ask Him to love that person through us. We can rest in the promise that when we ask we will receive, that our joy may be complete (see John 16:24).

CHAPTER 15
THROUGH EYES OF FAITH
CELEBRATION

*Did I not tell you that if you believed,
you would see the glory of God?*
—John 11:40

WHEN SAINT JOHN wrote the fourth gospel, he decided
to use one crucial incident in Jesus' ministry to serve as a
prologue to the account of the resurrection. He told the
story of Lazarus, who lived with his two sisters, Martha and Mary,
in the little village of Bethany. This family frequently extended their
hospitality to Jesus and the Twelve, and Jesus often visited them. It
is possible they were originally from Galilee, and if so, whenever
Jesus went to their house, He would have gotten a taste of home.
It's obvious they were special and close to His heart.

So it happened that when Lazarus suddenly became very sick,
the sisters did not feel it was presumptuous to ask Jesus to make a
house call. They sent an urgent message to Him that said, "Lord,
the one you love is sick" (John 11:3). Notice they didn't say, "Our
brother, Lazarus, who loves You to pieces, is sick." Instead, they
said, "Our brother whom *You* love is sick." During those extreme
moments in our lives, we can't approach the Lord claiming how
great our love is for Him, because it isn't. All we can do is count
on His love for us.

61

When Jesus received the message, He said, "This sickness will not end in death. No, it is for God's glory so that God's Son may be glorified through it" (verse 4). Then He stayed where He was for *two more days*. He didn't immediately journey to Bethany. Why? Because Jesus responded to God's timing, not human timing. He waited until just the right moment, and then He announced to His disciples, "Our friend Lazarus has fallen asleep; but I am going there to wake him up" (verse 11).

The disciples misunderstood what He said to them. "Lord," they replied, "if he sleeps, he will get better." After all, they reasoned, sleep is good for people who are sick.

So Jesus said plainly to them, "Lazarus is dead" (verses 12, 14).

After this, they journeyed back into Judaea—back into the crosshairs of Jesus' enemies who waited for Him. They returned because Jesus had something of inestimable importance to show them: the power and glory of God.

When they arrived, Jesus was told that Lazarus was dead and buried. Jesus had shown up 'too little and too late.' As soon as Martha heard about Jesus' arrival, she rushed out to meet Him. I think she felt frustrated, angry, and bitter. After all, if you were to call a doctor and leave word for him to call back, and he didn't bother to return your call, you would feel slighted as well. That was some sort of negligence. Jesus had let down each member of the family—especially Lazarus.

"Lord," Martha said to Jesus, "if you had been here, my brother would not have died." In others words, she was telling Jesus that if He had come when they called, their brother, Lazarus, would still be alive.

Jesus said, "Your brother will rise again."

"I know he will rise again in the resurrection at the last day," Martha countered (verses 21, 23-24). Many preachers remark that her response was pious, but I hear sarcasm in her voice, as if to say, "That promise at the end of time doesn't help us now, does it?"

But Jesus responded with wonderful words of assurance: "I am the resurrection, and the life: he that believeth in me, though he were dead, yet shall he live: and whosoever liveth and believeth in me shall never die" (John 11:25-26, KJV).

After this, Jesus accompanied Lazarus's family and friends to his grave. "Take away the stone," he commanded. Martha did not think that would be a good idea, as by now he had been dead for four days, and his body was decomposing. But Jesus said firmly, "Did I not tell you that if you believed, you would see the glory of God?" (verses 39-40). So they rolled away the stone.

When this had been done, Jesus prayed, "Father, I thank you that you have heard me." He first thanked God for listening, even though as of yet no response had been given and no miracle had occurred. Then He called in a loud voice—His divine summons, "Lazarus, come out!" (verses 41,43). Perhaps there was a long silence. Then, suddenly, before the eyes of the shocked crowd, a dead man shuffled out of the tomb.

It's interesting that Jesus told Martha that if she believed, she would see the glory of God (see John 11:40). That's usually the opposite of the way we think. We go by the philosophy that seeing is believing. But Jesus turned this around and said believing is seeing. In other words, we *believe* first, and then we *see* the glory of God.

It reminds me of those 3-D Magic Eye books. When you flip through the pages, they all look like a cluster of flat, two-dimensional floral prints and patterns.[1] But if you hold that picture about six inches from your eyes, slowly extend your arms, and look *through* the painting instead of *at* it—without focusing on it—the image jumps out at you. What has up to this time been two-dimensional is now three-dimensional.

Jesus' disciples had something of this experience. At first, they saw Him as just a man. For three years, they studied Him, observed Him, and looked hard *at* Him. But eventually, they began to look *through* Him with eyes of faith, and when they did they saw the face of God. Something three-dimensional became multi-dimensional. As Jesus had said in the Sermon on the Mount, "Blessed are the pure in heart: for they shall see God" (Matt. 5:8, KJV). First comes faith, and then comes the vision.

This was certainly true of Simon Peter. When he left fishing to become a disciple, he most likely viewed Jesus as a prophet, a healer, an exorcist, a miracle-worker, and a teacher. However, he came to the place where he could confess that Jesus was "the Christ, the Son of the living God" (Matt. 16:16). Then came the humiliation of the crucifixion, and Peter's highest hopes for Jesus fell apart like sandcastles. When the women who went to the tomb reported to the disciples that Jesus had risen from the dead, "they did not believe the women, because their words seemed to them like nonsense" (Luke 24:11). But then Simon Peter met the risen Christ, and in that moment He became more to Peter than he had ever imagined.

For this reason on the day of Pentecost, Peter could rise to address the crowd that had gathered outside and tell them what he now saw through eyes of faith:

> Men of Israel, listen to this: Jesus of Nazareth was a man accredited by God to you by miracles, wonders and signs, which God did among you through him, as you yourselves know. This man was handed over to you by God's set purpose and foreknowledge; and you, with the help of wicked men, put him to death by nailing him to the cross. But God raised him from the dead, freeing him from the agony of death, because it was impossible for death to keep its hold on him.
>
> —Acts 2:22-24

Whereas once Peter had rebuked Jesus for saying He must be killed and on the third day be raised to life (see Matthew 16:21-22), he could now affirm that Jesus' excruciating death as a common criminal was all part of God's plan—and Jesus' subsequent resurrection was a vindication of that plan. Peter concluded, "Therefore let all Israel be assured of this: God has made this Jesus, whom you crucified, both Lord and Christ" (Acts 2:36). Peter saw Jesus in a brand new way: through eyes of faith. So must we.

Believing *is* seeing. Huston Smith wrote, "Faith is believing what you do not see, and the reward of faith is seeing what you believe."[2]

EPILOGUE

IN THE MIDST of all the glitz and glamour of the holidays, we become aware of another level of experience—of a vertical dimension in life. We squint and stare. We sense the unseen Presence. In that sacred moment, we realize it is not the holiday we are celebrating, but the Christ. Amen.

ENDNOTES

Chapter 1: Thankful in *All* Circumstances? (Thanksgiving)
1. Hannah Whitall Smith, *The God of All Comfort* (Chicago: Moody Press, 1956 edition), pp. 247-249.
2. Paul Lee Tan, Th.D., *Encyclopedia of 7,700 Illustrations*, #659 "Him, Him, Him," *American Holiness Journal* (Rockville, MD: Assurance Publishers, 1979), p. 239.

Chapter 3: How Does The Savior Come? (Advent)
1. Fanny J. Crosby (1820–1915), "Pass Me Not, O Gentle Savior," verse 1 (written 1868).
2. Walter B. Knight, *Knight's Treasury of Illustrations*, "A Christ Who Shines in Darkness" (Grand Rapids, MI: Wm. B. Eerdmans Publishing Company, 1963), p. 203.

Chapter 4: I Believe (Christmas)
1. The title of this chapter is also the title of a book by Helmut Thielicke, *I Believe* (Philadelphia, PA: Fortress Press, 1968).
2. Thielicke, *op. cit.*, pp. 74-75.

Chapter 6: A New Beginning (New Year's Day)
1. John T. Seamands, *Dayspring: Daily Devotions from the Four Gospels* (Grand Rapids, MI: Francis Asbury Press, 1989), pp. 9-10.

2. Edgar T. Chrisemer, *Every Common Bush* (Boston, MA: Bruce Humphries, Inc., 1953), p. 19.

Chapter 8: A Consecrated Life (Ash Wednesday)
1. Catherine Jackson, *The Christian's Secret of a Happy Life for Today: A Paraphrase of Hannah Whitall Smith's Classic* (Minneapolis, MN: World Wide Publications, 1979), pp. 41-42.
2. Adelaide A. Pollard, "Have Thine Own Way, Lord," verse 1 (written 1902, based on Jeremiah 18:6).
3. Jackson, *op. cit.*, pp. 39-40
4. Henry T. Blackabay and Claude V. King, *Experiencing God: How to Live the Full Adventure of Knowing and Doing the Will of God* (Nashville, TN: Broadman & Holman Publishers, 1994), pp. 45-46.

Chapter 9: Simple Acts of Kindness (Lent)
1. Jack Canfield and Mark Victor Hansen, *Chicken Soup for The Soul: 101 Stories To Open The Heart and Rekindle The Spirit* (Deerfield Beach, Florida: Health Communications, Inc., 1993) "The Gift," p. 24.
2. Maxie Dunnam, *Perceptions: Observations on Everyday Life* (Wilmore, KY: Bristol Books, 1990) "Someone Always Forgets," p. 67 (story told originally by Halford Luccock).
3. This took place at the Innabah Program Center, Spring City, Pennsylvania, in July 2009.

Chapter 10: The Gift of Atonement (Passion Sunday)
1. Maxie Dunnam, *This Is Christianity* (Nashville, TN: Abingdon Press, 1994), p. 54.
2. Horatio Spafford (1828–1888), "It Is Well with My Soul," verse 3 (written 1873).
3. Charlotte Elliott, "Just As I Am," verses 1 and 6 (written 1835).

Chapter 11: The Anointed One (Palm Sunday)
1. Adapted from Joe A. Harding, *Christian Clippings* (Hudson, FL, April 1981), p. 19.

2. D. Guthrie and J.A. Motyer, eds., *The New Bible Commentary Revised* (Grand Rapids, MI: Wm. B. Eerdmans Publishing Company, 1970), p. 955.
3. Warren W. Wiersbe, *The Bible Exposition Commentary*, vol. 1 (Wheaton, IL: Victor Books, 1989), p. 339.
4. Georg Weissel, "Lift up Your Heads, Ye Mighty Gates," verses 1, 2 and 3 (written 1642, translated by Catherine Winkworth, 1855). Based on Psalm 24.

Chapter 12: Why Weep? (Easter)
1. Augustus M. Toplady, "Rock of Ages," verses 1, 2 and 3 (written 1776).
2. Corrie ten Boom with John and Elizabeth Sherrill, *The Hiding Place* (Old Tappan, NJ: Fleming H. Revell Company, 1971), pp. 34, 38.
3. Ibid., p. 39.

Chapter 13: A Meal between Friends (Eastertide)
1. Fred H. Wight, *Manners and Customs of Bible Lands* (Chicago: Moody Press, 1953), pp. 76-77.
2. Ibid., p. 78.
3. Ibid.
4. Ibid., pp. 78-79, referencing George H. Scherer, *The Eastern Color of the Bible* (Old Tappan, NJ: Fleming H. Revell, no date).

Chapter 14: The Fire That Fell (Pentecost)
1. Charles Wesley, "O Thou Who Camest from Above," verses 1 and 2 (written 1762).
2. Michael P. Green, ed., *Illustrations for Biblical Preaching*, illustration # 154, "Christian Life, Source of" (Grand Rapids, MI: Baker Book House, 1989), p. 55.

Chapter 15: Through Eyes of Faith (Celebration)
1. This type of picture is referred to as a "stereogram." Magic Eye, Inc. and Marc Grossman, O.D., L. Ac., *Magic Eye: Beyond 3D* (Kansas City, MO: Andrews McMeel Publishing, 2004), p. 5.
2. Huston Smith, "Why Faith Matters Today," *Guideposts* (Carmel, New York), pp. 33-35. Used with permission.

To order additional copies of this book,
please visit www.redemption-press.com
Also available on Amazon.com and BarnesandNoble.com
Or by calling toll free 1+ (844) 273-3336

CPSIA information can be obtained
at www.ICGtesting.com
Printed in the USA
FFOW02n0335110215
10971FF

9 781632 320360